Guide to Friendship

Understanding the friendship between people and improving relationships

Albert Olwer

Guide to friendships

1.Friendship

Friendship is a fundamental value in everyone's life. It can be defined as an emotional bond that develops between two people based on mutual sympathy, trust, understanding, and mutual support. The importance of friendship in a person's life is crucial, as it represents one of the pillars on which to build human relationships and emotional well-being.

Friendship is a bond that goes beyond blood ties and family relationships, as it is a conscious choice to share emotions, feelings, and life moments with a person one esteems and appreciates. It allows us to experience meaningful and intense moments, enriching our existence and adding value to our days.

One of the most important aspects of friendship is the ability to be able to confide in someone who understands us, accepts us for who we are, and supports us at all times. Friends are those with whom we can share our joys and sorrows, our successes and failures, without fear of being judged or rejected. The presence of a friend gives us the security of being able to rely on someone who supports us in difficult times and celebrates our victories with us.

Friendship helps to develop a sense of belonging and identity, as a friend represents a significant part of our life and our history. Sharing experiences and moments with a friend allows us to build unforgettable memories that enrich our emotional baggage and help us grow as individuals.

Furthermore, friendship helps to overcome loneliness and emotional isolation, offering constant and unconditional support. A friend is someone who knows how to listen without judgment, how to comfort without words, and how to be present even in moments of silence and difficulty. Thanks to friendship, we feel less alone in the world and have the certainty that there is someone we can count on in every situation.

Finally, friendship is a value that helps us grow and improve as individuals. Friends encourage us to bring out the best in ourselves, motivate us to overcome our limits, and encourage us to pursue our dreams. With a friend by our side, we have the opportunity to explore new horizons, expand our mental horizons, and discover sides of ourselves we did not know.

Friendship is an indispensable value in everyone's life. It enriches us emotionally, supports us in difficult times, helps us overcome loneliness, and encourages us to grow and improve as individuals. Cultivating and preserving the friendships that surround us is therefore essential for our psychological well-being and happiness. Let us never forget to show gratitude and appreciation towards our friends, as they represent a precious treasure that enriches our lives in a unique and irreplaceable way.

2. Characteristics of the ideal friend

The ideal friend is the kind of person who makes you feel comfortable, understood, and accepted for who you are. They are a constant presence in your life, always ready to listen, support, and share happy and difficult moments with you. But what are the characteristics that truly define the ideal friend?

First of all, an ideal friend is an authentic and sincere person. This means they are honest, open, and transparent with you and others. They do not hide the truth or lie to make themselves look better, but are always sincere in their words and actions. This sincerity creates a solid foundation of trust on which to build your friendship, making it resilient to difficulties and the tests of time.

Another fundamental characteristic of the ideal friend is empathy. This means being able to put yourself in the other person's shoes, understand their emotions, concerns, and needs. An empathetic friend is a attentive listener, capable of offering comfort, support, and understanding when you need it. They can read between the lines and pick up on your feelings even when you do not express them clearly, making you feel truly understood and appreciated.

Furthermore, the ideal friend is an endless source of positivity and good humor. They are the kind of person who can make you laugh even in the most difficult moments, give you hope and optimism when all seems lost. Their positive energy infects everyone around them, creating an atmosphere of joy and lightness that makes you feel good and peaceful. With them, every day is an adventure to face with enthusiasm and cheerfulness.

But it is not only their good humor that characterizes the ideal friend. They are also a compassionate and caring person, who sincerely cares about your well-being and happiness. They are the person who asks you how you really are, who is interested in your needs and desires, who is willing to go the extra mile to help you and make you feel loved. Thanks to this constant care and attention, you always feel supported and protected, even in the most complicated moments of life.

Moreover, the ideal friend is a constant and reliable presence in your life. They are the person you can count on in any circumstance, who never abandons you and is always there for you, even when others turn their backs on you. You can call them at any time of day or night, knowing they will answer your call and help you with any problem you may have. This consistency and reliability is what truly makes the ideal friend special, because it makes you feel safe and protected, as if you have a guardian angel always by your side.

Lastly, the ideal friend is the kind of person

who helps you grow and become a better version of yourself. They encourage you to push past your limits, pursue your dreams, explore new paths and opportunities. They urge you to be your best self, to fight for what you believe in, to be brave and determined in your choices. With them, you learn what it truly means to be yourself, to live each day with authenticity and passion, to give your best in every situation.

The ideal friend is a unique combination of sincerity, empathy, positivity, care, consistency, and personal growth. They are a unique and irreplaceable person who makes you feel safe, loved, and appreciated in every moment of your life. Those who are fortunate enough to have a friend like this know how precious and rare this person is, and would do anything to keep them by their side forever. An ideal friend is a treasure to be cherished, a light that guides your path and makes you feel truly lucky and privileged.

3. The search for the ideal friend most akin to us

The search for the ideal friend is often a difficult and complex task, as each of us has different needs, desires, and personalities that make it challenging to find someone who fully understands who we are and can share moments of joy and difficulty with us. However, there are some places and ways in which we can approach individuals who could become our closest friends and who could accompany our lives with sincere friendship and support.

One of the places where we can look for the ideal friend most akin to us is within the social circles to which we belong. These can be sports clubs, cultural associations, volunteer groups, or training courses. Being part of an environment where common interests and passions are shared can promote the creation of deep and meaningful bonds with people who share our same visions and values.

Furthermore, actively participating in these activities allows us to get to know others better and show them who we really are, thus fostering the development of authentic and lasting relationships.

Another place to look for the ideal friend most akin to us is within our existing circles of friendships. Often, our friends know our strengths, weaknesses, and deepest desires better than anyone else, and they may be able to introduce us to people who could become our closest friends. Additionally, sharing new experiences and interests with the friends we already have can expand our social circle and allow us to meet new and interesting individuals who could enrich our lives with their presence and friendship.

Another way to search for the ideal friend most akin to us is through social media and online platforms. The internet has made the world smaller and has allowed us to connect with people from all over the globe, offering the opportunity to meet individuals who share our same interests and passions even from a distance. Through themed groups, discussion forums, and dating sites, it is possible to connect with people who could become our closest friends with whom we can share not only common interests but also life experiences and emotions.

Finally, another way to search for the ideal friend most akin to us is through volunteering and solidarity activities. Participating in social and humanitarian initiatives allows us not only to use our skills to serve others but also to connect with individuals who share our sensitivity and worldview. Additionally, helping others and sharing moments of difficulty and joy with strangers can foster the creation of deep and authentic bonds that can evolve into lasting and meaningful friendships.

The search for the ideal friend most akin to us is a complex and engaging journey that requires time, commitment, and openness to others. Exploring different places and ways to meet new people and expand our social circle can offer the opportunity to meet individuals who can become our closest friends, capable of accompanying us in life with sincerity, understanding, and affection. It is important to remain open and willing to welcome new people and experiences into our lives, as the ideal friend may be just around the corner, ready to share moments of happiness and camaraderie with us.

4. How to develop meaningful friendships

Developing meaningful friendships is a process that requires time, commitment, and sincerity. It's not just about meeting people and forming shallow connections, but about creating deep and lasting connections with individuals who share our values, interests, and life goals. Meaningful friendships enrich us, support us, and help us grow as individuals, and are essential for our emotional and mental well-being.

To develop meaningful friendships, it is important to be authentic and open with others. Showing up as your true self and sharing your thoughts, feelings, and experiences sincerely helps create a deeper bond with the people around you. Transparency and honesty are the foundation of any meaningful relationship, and only through genuineness can solid and lasting bonds be built.

Furthermore, to develop meaningful friendships it is important to be empathetic and compassionate towards others. Being willing to listen and support our friends in times of difficulty, showing understanding and support when needed, are gestures that strengthen the bond and create a solid foundation for an authentic and meaningful relationship. Empathy is the ability to put oneself in the shoes of others, to understand their emotions and needs, and to respond with sensitivity and kindness.

Additionally, to develop meaningful friendships it is important to invest time and energy in relationships. Friendships are not built overnight, but require constant commitment, dedication, and attention. Spending quality time with our friends, sharing experiences and special moments together, helps strengthen the bond and solidify the relationship over time. The aspect of sharing is fundamental in establishing a stable and lasting friendship.

Furthermore, to develop meaningful friendships it is important to cultivate common interests and passions. Finding people who share our passions, hobbies, and favorite activities helps create a deeper and more authentic bond. Sharing experiences and special moments related to our common interests allows us to create memorable memories and strengthen the bond with our friends. Sharing common passions and interests is a great way to create a common ground on which to build a meaningful relationship.

Moreover, to develop meaningful friendships it is important to be available and present for our friends. Being present in the lives of others, showing interest and attention to their needs and desires, is crucial for building an authentic and supportive relationship. Being available to support our friends in times of difficulty, to celebrate with them the successes and joys of life, is essential to keep the bond alive and strengthen the relationship over time.

Additionally, to develop meaningful friendships it is important to be patient and tolerant with others. Every person is unique and has their own path, strengths and weaknesses, fears and insecurities. Being patient and understanding towards others allows us to create an environment of trust and mutual respect, and to build a healthy and meaningful relationship. Tolerance is the ability to accept and respect the differences of others, to understand their perspectives, and to respond with kindness and an open heart.

Moreover, to develop meaningful friendships it is important to overcome the difficulties and differences that may arise along the way. Every relationship has its ups and downs, its challenges and difficulties to face.
Overcoming difficulties together, dealing with problems with maturity and an open heart, is essential to keep the relationship alive and strengthen the bond over time. Difficulties can

test the strength of a friendship, but overcoming them together strengthens the bond and makes the relationship deeper and more authentic.

Finally, to develop meaningful friendships it is important to be grateful for the people who play an important role in our lives. Showing gratitude and appreciation for our friends, for the support and affection they show us, is essential to keep the bond alive and strengthen the relationship over time. Gratitude is a powerful feeling that allows us to appreciate the people who have a positive impact on our lives, to recognize the value of meaningful relationships, and to cultivate mutual love and affection.

Developing meaningful friendships is a process that requires commitment, dedication, and authenticity. Creating deep and lasting connections with the people around us enriches us, supports us, and helps us grow as individuals. Being authentic, empathetic, available, patient, and tolerant, cultivating common interests and sharing special moments together are key elements in building meaningful and lasting friendships. Showing gratitude and appreciation for our friends, overcoming difficulties and differences together, are gestures that strengthen the bond and make the relationship deeper and more authentic. Meaningful friendships are a precious treasure that must be nurtured with care and respect, and that accompany us along our life journey.

5.Communicating effectively with friends

Communicating effectively with friends is crucial for maintaining healthy and lasting relationships. Communication plays a fundamental role in interpersonal relationships, as it allows us to express our emotions, opinions, and thoughts clearly and honestly. However, it is not always easy to communicate effectively with friends, as misunderstandings, misinterpretations, or communication problems may arise. In this article, we will explore some strategies and techniques for communicating effectively with friends, in order to maintain positive and satisfying relationships.

First of all, it is important to be aware of your communication style. Each person has a unique way of expressing themselves and interacting with others, and understanding your communication style can help improve the quality of your relationships with friends. For example, some people may be more direct and assertive in communication, while others may be more passive or diplomatic. Knowing your communication style can help you understand how you are perceived by others and make any necessary corrections or adjustments to communicate more effectively.

Furthermore, it is important to be aware of your nonverbal communication. Nonverbal communication, which includes gestures, facial expressions, posture, and tone of voice, can convey powerful messages and influence how others perceive us. For instance, a calm and relaxed tone of voice can convey confidence and tranquility, while a loud or aggressive tone of voice can create tension and conflict. Paying attention to your nonverbal communication can help ensure that the message you are sending is consistent with your intentions and is received positively by friends.

To communicate effectively with friends, it is also important to be empathetic and listen actively. Being empathetic means being able to put yourself in the other person's shoes, understand their emotions, concerns, and perspectives. Empathy is crucial for establishing an emotional connection with friends and demonstrating respect and understanding towards them. Active listening, on the other hand, means being present in the moment and fully focusing on what the other person is saying, without interruptions or distractions. Active listening allows you to pick up on both verbal and nonverbal cues from the other person, show interest, and respond appropriately.

Furthermore, to communicate effectively with friends, it is important to be clear, concise, and direct. Expressing your ideas and opinions clearly and unequivocally can reduce the risk of misunderstandings and misinterpretations. Using simple and direct language, avoiding ambiguous or ambivalent phrases, can contribute to more effective and transparent communication. Additionally, it is important to be respectful and non-judgmental in communication with friends, even when expressing different opinions or addressing sensitive topics. Showing respect and acceptance for others' opinions can foster a climate of trust and openness in relationships with friends.

Finally, to communicate effectively with friends, it is also important to be willing to resolve any conflicts or misunderstandings. Conflicts and differences of opinion are part of human relationships and can present opportunities for growth and learning. Addressing conflicts constructively, listening to the other person's opinions, expressing your emotions, and seeking shared solutions can strengthen bonds with friends and overcome communication barriers. The ability to manage conflicts empathetically, tolerantly, and assertively can be a valuable resource for maintaining healthy and fulfilling relationships with friends.

Being aware of your communication style,

nonverbal communication, being empathetic and listening actively, being clear, concise, and direct, and being willing to resolve conflicts are some of the strategies and techniques that can help improve the quality of communication with friends. Effective communication requires practice, commitment, and an open mind, but it can lead to more authentic, meaningful, and rewarding relationships with friends.

6. Resolving conflicts in friendships

Friendships are an important part of everyone's life. Whether they are long-standing friendships or more recent ones, conflicts can arise in any type of relationship. Resolving conflicts in friendships is essential for maintaining healthy and lasting relationships.

Conflicts in friendships can have many causes. They can stem from misunderstandings, jealousy, differing opinions, or different goals. Whatever the cause of the conflict, it is important to address it in a constructive manner in order to continue enjoying a healthy and positive friendship.

In many cases, conflicts in friendships can be resolved by openly and honestly talking with the other person involved. It is crucial to communicate your feelings clearly, express your concerns, and listen to the opinions and feelings of your friend. Open and honest communication is essential for addressing conflicts and finding a solution that satisfies both parties.

In some cases, it may be helpful to involve a neutral third party, such as a mediator or counselor, to help resolve the conflict peacefully and constructively. This person can assist in facilitating communication between the parties, helping them find common ground and work together to overcome their differences.

One key to resolving conflicts in friendships is the ability to empathize and try to understand the other person's perspective. It is important to accept that everyone has a different viewpoint and that each person's experiences and feelings are valid. Being empathetic and respectful towards the other person is crucial for building and maintaining a healthy friendship.

Additionally, it is important to be willing to compromise and work together to find a solution that is fair and satisfactory for both parties. Sometimes, sacrifices or changes in behavior may be necessary to effectively resolve conflicts. The important thing is to be open to dialogue and collaboration to find a solution that is acceptable to both.

Another useful strategy for resolving conflicts in friendships is to try to address problems as soon as possible. Ignoring conflicts or hoping they will resolve on their own often worsens the situation and leads to escalating tensions and animosity. Confronting issues head-on and seeking a solution together is the best way to overcome conflicts and strengthen the bond of friendship.

Lastly, it is important to learn to forgive and let go of past offenses. Holding onto grudges or resentment can make it difficult to resolve conflicts and can hinder the restoration of trust and loyalty between friends. Learning to forgive and let go can help heal past wounds and build a stronger and more solid relationship.

Resolving conflicts in friendships can be challenging, but it is also an opportunity for growth and strengthening relationships with others. Addressing problems openly, communicating effectively, and working together to find a solution can lead to greater understanding and mutual respect. Maintaining a positive and open attitude helps overcome difficulties and build lasting and meaningful friendships.

7.The Importance of Being a Good Friend

Being a good friend is one of the most important things we can do in life. Friendship is a special bond that connects us to someone in a deep and meaningful way. A good friend is someone we can rely on at any time, someone who supports us, encourages us, and helps us overcome life's challenges.

Being a good friend means being present, listening, and understanding others. It means being empathetic, kind, and caring. A good friend is someone who loves us unconditionally, accepts us for who we are, and supports us in times of difficulty.

The importance of being a good friend lies in the fact that friendship is one of the most precious things we can have in life. Friends are like a chosen family, and they are a source of joy, comfort, and support in every situation.

Being a good friend also comes with responsibilities. It means being honest and sincere, being there when our friends need us, and being willing to help them in any way possible. It means being present in happy moments and sad moments, being a attentive listener and an unwavering support.

A good friend is someone who is always there for you, who supports and encourages you, who makes you laugh and comforts you when you're sad. A good friend is someone who accepts you for who you are, with your faults and weaknesses, and loves you nonetheless.

Being a good friend has numerous benefits, both for the giver and the receiver of friendship. Studies show that people with close and solid friendships are happier, healthier, and more satisfied with their lives. Friendship is an antidote to loneliness and stress, and it can help us overcome adversity more easily.

Being a good friend makes us better people. They teach us the importance of being generous, compassionate, and caring towards others. They teach us to be more open and loving, and help us grow and evolve as individuals.

The importance of being a good friend is also reflected in our relationships with others. Being a good friend helps us to be more empathetic and understanding towards others, to be more tolerant and open in our interpersonal relationships.

Being a good friend is one of the most important things we can do in life. Friendship is a precious treasure that enriches our lives and helps us overcome life's challenges. Being a good friend involves responsibility, kindness, and unconditional love. Being a good friend makes us better people and helps us live a happier and more fulfilling life. If you have a good friend, appreciate and cherish them, because friendship is a priceless gift.

8. The balance between online and offline friendships

We live in a digital era where personal relationships can be cultivated both offline and online. Friendships are an essential element of each of our lives and are crucial for our emotional and psychological well-being. But how can we find a healthy balance between our offline and online friendships?

Offline friendships are those formed face to face, through physical meetings and direct interactions. These relationships are rooted in tangible reality and offer a sense of deeper and more authentic connection. Offline friendships can include long-time friends, family members, coworkers, or people met casually in everyday life. These relationships are characterized by shared moments, direct experiences, and a physical presence that can be reassuring and rewarding.

On the other hand, online friendships develop through digital platforms such as social media, discussion forums, chat rooms, and messaging apps. These relationships can be based on common interests, chance encounters, or connections through mutual friends. Online friendships offer the opportunity to connect with people from all over the world, share specific interests, and find support and understanding in times of need.

Both forms of friendship have their own advantages and challenges. Offline friendships offer more immediate and intimate contact, allowing people to establish deeper and lasting bonds. However, they can also be limited by physical distance, personal commitments, and people's availability. Online friendships, on the other hand, can be more flexible and accessible, allowing people to connect anytime and anywhere. However, they may lack the warmth and empathy of face-to-face interactions and may be more prone to misunderstandings and superficiality.

To find a healthy balance between online and offline friendships, it is important to consider your emotional, social, and psychological needs. Offline friendships can offer more immediate and tangible support, while online friendships can broaden social circles and offer opportunities for diverse connection and sharing.

Here are some tips for successfully managing your friendships in both contexts:

1. Value the diversity of your relationships: try to maintain a balance between offline and online friendships, seeking to make the most of both types of connections. Each of them can offer different perspectives, new learning opportunities, and moments of joy and support.

2. Create shared experiences: try to find ways to integrate your online and offline friendships by organizing social events, outings, or

activities that involve both the people you meet in person and those you know online. This will allow you to create stronger and more authentic bonds based on shared experiences and meaningful moments.

3. Maintain a balance between time spent online and offline: try to dedicate time to face-to-face relationships, enjoying the company of your friends and sharing real-life moments. Similarly, do not neglect your online friendships, maintaining regular contact and actively participating in online conversations and activities.

4. Choose carefully the people with whom you establish meaningful connections: whether it is online or offline friendships, it is important to carefully select the people with whom you want to establish deeper and more meaningful connections. Try to identify people who share your values, interests, and goals, and who inspire and support you in your personal growth journey.

5. Communicate openly and honestly: communication is essential to maintaining healthy and meaningful relationships, both online and offline. Be honest in your interactions, express your thoughts, feelings, and needs clearly and respectfully, and listen carefully to the opinions and emotions of others. Open and honest communication can help resolve any conflicts, strengthen existing bonds, and promote the growth and development of relationships.

6. Respect personal boundaries and limits: it is important to respect the boundaries and personal limits of others, whether they are online or offline friends. Seek consent before sharing private information or sensitive photos, respect people's communication timing and rhythms, and be mindful of people's sensitivities towards certain topics or situations. Mutual respect is essential for building healthy and lasting relationships.

Finding a balance between online and offline friendships can enrich our social life and improve our emotional and psychological well-being. Whether it's with long-time friends, family members, or people we meet casually in our daily lives, or whether it's with individuals we connect with through digital platforms, each of these relationships has the potential to enrich our existence and offer valuable emotional and social support. Maintaining a healthy balance between online and offline friendships allows us to fully enjoy all the opportunities for connection and sharing that life has to offer, contributing to our sense of belonging, happiness, and personal fulfillment.

9. How to deal with loneliness and lack of friends

Loneliness and lack of friends are very common feelings that can arise at different times in a person's life. There are many reasons why a person may feel lonely or have few friends, including moving to new cities, changes in personal or professional life, difficulties in making new friendships, or simply because many people prefer to spend time alone.

Regardless of the circumstances that lead to loneliness, it is important to address this emotional state in a healthy and constructive way. Loneliness can have negative effects on a person's mental health and emotional well-being, so it is essential to find ways to address and overcome it.

One of the first things to do when facing loneliness is to accept it and understand that it is normal to feel this way from time to time. Each of us needs moments of solitude to recharge and reconnect with ourselves. However, it is also important to be aware when loneliness becomes excessive and starts to have a negative impact on our lives.

To address loneliness and lack of friends, it is important to seek positive ways to socialize and create new connections. There are many activities and strategies that can be adopted to meet new people and build new friendships. Firstly, it is important to participate in social events and activities that interest us. This can include courses, clubs, interest groups, cultural or sports events, etc. Engaging in these activities allows us to meet people with similar interests and create new connections.

Furthermore, it is important to be open and available to make new friends. Often, loneliness can make us feel shy or insecure in relating to others. However, it is important to overcome these barriers and open up to new people we meet. Being friendly, sociable, and empathetic can help create meaningful connections with others and build new friendships.

The internet can be a valuable ally in the fight against loneliness and lack of friends. There are numerous social networking sites and apps that allow us to meet new people and make new friends. Participating in online forums, interest groups, and virtual communities can be a great way to socialize and connect with people from around the world. Additionally, there are also sites and apps specifically designed to help people make new friends, such as Meetup, Bumble BFF, or Couchsurfing.

Beyond the more practical approaches to dealing with loneliness and lack of friends, it is also important to work on oneself to improve self-esteem and confidence in relationships with others. Working on healthy and positive habits, such as exercising, eating well, getting enough sleep, and managing stress, can help maintain a healthy and balanced mind. Additionally, it is important to dedicate time to activities that we enjoy and make us happy, such as reading, painting, playing sports, cooking, etc. This allows us to relax, recharge, and connect with ourselves.

Finally, it is crucial to seek help when needed. If loneliness and lack of friends become too heavy to bear, it is important to seek support from friends, family, or mental health professionals. Talking about our emotions and sharing our experiences can help us feel less alone and find solutions to address the situation in a healthy and positive way. Loneliness and lack of friends can be difficult feelings to deal with, but it is possible to overcome them with commitment, determination, and a bit of creativity. Seeking positive ways to socialize, working on oneself, and asking for help when needed are crucial steps to address loneliness and build a meaningful social support network. Let us always remember that we are capable of making new friends and building connections that enrich our lives.

10. Maintaining a healthy and lasting friendship

Maintaining a healthy and lasting friendship is a goal that many of us strive to achieve. Friendship is a special bond that is cultivated over time and requires commitment from both parties. However, it is not always easy to maintain a healthy and lasting friendship, as conflicts, misunderstandings, and changes in the lives of both individuals can arise. In this article, we will explore some strategies and tips on how to maintain a healthy and lasting friendship, addressing challenges and strengthening the bond.

First and foremost, it is important to understand that friendships, like any other relationship, require commitment and dedication from both parties involved. It is crucial to be open to communication, to listen and understand each other's needs. Communication is key to addressing conflicts and overcoming any misunderstandings that may arise in the course of the relationship.

One of the first rules for maintaining a healthy and lasting friendship is honesty. It is essential to be honest with oneself and with the friend about one's feelings, expectations, and boundaries. Maintaining a friendship based on mutual trust and transparency is essential to building a stable and lasting relationship over time.

Furthermore, it is important to respect the individuality and autonomy of the friend. Each of us has our own interests, passions, and life projects, and it is important to allow the other person to explore and cultivate their own passions. Respecting the desires and choices of the friend is essential to maintaining a healthy and balanced friendship, avoiding imposing one's own opinions or expectations.

Another fundamental aspect of maintaining a

healthy and lasting friendship is empathy. Being able to put oneself in the other person's shoes, to understand their emotions and needs, is essential for building an empathetic and supportive relationship. Being present in difficult times, supporting the friend in moments of distress, and celebrating together in moments of happiness are gestures that strengthen the bond and consolidate the friendship over time.

It is also important to dedicate time to the relationship and to maintaining the friendship bond. Too often, as the years go by and professional and family commitments increase, there is a risk of neglecting the friendship and not dedicating enough time and attention to the other person. It is essential to organize moments of sharing, laughter, and leisure together, to strengthen the bond and keep the friendship relationship alive over time.

Finally, it is important to be flexible and adapt

to the changes that life and circumstances bring in the friendship relationship. People grow, change, and evolve over time, and it is important to be open to the changes and transformations that can influence the friendship relationship. Being willing to accept differences, tolerate disagreements, and adapt to new scenarios is essential for maintaining a healthy and lasting friendship over time.

Being able to communicate openly, listen with empathy, respect the other person's individuality, dedicate time to the relationship, and adapt to changes are the keys to building a solid and empathetic relationship over time. Friendship is a precious treasure to cultivate and preserve, and by following these tips, one can strengthen the bond and keep the friendship relationship alive over the years.

11. Letting go of negative friendships

Not all friendships are positive and healthy. Sometimes, we find ourselves dealing with negative friendships that make us feel bad, put us in difficult situations, or drag us down. In these cases, it is important to learn to let go of these negative friendships in order to make space for more positive and beneficial relationships for ourselves.

The first step in letting go of a negative friendship is recognizing that it is not good for us. Often, we are inclined to justify certain behaviors or attitudes of friends who hurt us, thinking that it is just a temporary phase or that we can help them change. However, it is essential to understand that we cannot change others and that people must want to change themselves. If a friendship constantly makes us feel sad, insecure, or frustrated, it is necessary to acknowledge this situation and decide to distance ourselves for our own good.

Once the decision to let go of a negative friendship has been made, it is important to act with determination and firmness. This means setting clear and firm boundaries with the person in question, communicating clearly and respectfully the reason why we are inclined to make this decision. It may not be easy, but it is essential for our emotional and psychological well-being. It is crucial to maintain our position and not be influenced by any pressures or attempts at manipulation by the friend we are trying to distance ourselves from.

In some cases, it may be necessary to permanently distance oneself from this person, removing them from our social media contacts or avoiding the same places where we used to meet. Although it may be painful, it is important to understand that it is not selfish to take care of ourselves and our emotions. Letting go of a negative friendship can be a difficult but necessary choice in order to make space for more positive and constructive relationships in our lives.

Once the decision to distance oneself from a negative friendship has been made, it is important to dedicate time to healing emotional wounds and working on self-esteem and self-worth. It may be helpful to talk to a therapist or psychologist to better understand the dynamics of a toxic relationship and learn to strengthen our ability to establish healthy boundaries and positive relationships.

Furthermore, it is important to seek the support of friends and family who care about us and support us in our decision to let go of a negative friendship. Having positive and loving people around us can help us overcome the pain and loss associated with the end of a toxic relationship and build a strong and constructive support network.

Letting go of a negative friendship may be a painful decision, but necessary for our emotional and psychological well-being. It is crucial to understand that taking care of ourselves and our emotions is not selfish, and that having genuine and positive relationships in our lives is important. With time and the help of friends and professionals, it is possible to overcome the pain associated with the end of a toxic friendship and build healthier and more fulfilling relationships for our emotional and psychological well-being.

12. Creating a supportive environment to find new friendships

Creating a supportive environment to find new friendships can be a stimulating and rewarding task. Social relationships are an integral part of everyone's life, and having a good circle of friends can bring joy, support, and a sense of belonging. However, it can be challenging for some people to find new friendships, especially if they are shy, introverted, or new to a particular city or environment. In these cases, it is important to create a supportive environment that can facilitate meeting and bonding with new people.

One of the first steps to create a supportive environment to find new friendships is to work on self-esteem. Feeling confident and aware of your own personal value can make a difference when trying to establish connections with others. Practicing self-compassion and self-acceptance can help combat social anxiety and show openness and availability towards others, creating a positive atmosphere that makes it easier to approach and get to know new people.

Another important aspect to consider is the ability to be empathetic and compassionate towards others. Interpersonal relationships are based on reciprocity and the ability to understand and listen to others. Being open, curious, and interested in the stories and experiences of others can help establish authentic and meaningful connections. Additionally, being kind, caring, and available towards others can create an atmosphere of trust and openness that facilitates the creation of new friendships.

Another way to create a supportive environment to find new friendships is to attend places and events where you have the opportunity to meet people with similar interests. Participating in classes, workshops, clubs, or associations can be a great way to meet people who share our passions and interests. In these contexts, it is easier to establish meaningful relationships and find people to share pleasant moments and experiences with.

In addition, leveraging online platforms and social media can be a great way to expand your social circle and find new friendships. Dating websites and apps are not only reserved for romantic encounters, but can also be used to meet new people and form friendships. Online groups and communities can be a virtual space to meet people with similar interests and create meaningful connections, which can then turn into real friendships in real life.

Another important aspect to consider when trying to create a supportive environment to find new friendships is the ability to be authentic and genuine with others. Showing yourself for who you truly are, without masks or filters, can be an effective way to attract authentic and sincere people into your life.

Being honest, transparent, and vulnerable can help create an atmosphere of trust and authenticity that promotes the creation of deep and lasting bonds.

Finally, one of the most important things to do when trying to create a supportive environment to find new friendships is to be patient and not have too high expectations. Building meaningful and lasting relationships takes time, commitment, and mutual trust. It is important to be patient and not get discouraged if initial relationship attempts do not go as hoped. Each encounter is an opportunity to learn something new about yourself and others, and can lead to the creation of authentic and lasting bonds over time.

In conclusion, creating a supportive environment to find new friendships can be a stimulating and rewarding process. Working on self-esteem, being empathetic and compassionate towards others, attending places and events where you have the opportunity to meet people with similar interests, leveraging online platforms and social media, being authentic and genuine with others, and being patient and not having too high expectations are all effective ways to foster the creation of meaningful and lasting connections with new people. Remembering that social relationships are important for the emotional and psychological well-being of everyone, it is essential to dedicate time and energy to building new friendships and nurturing the bonds that accompany us along the path of life.

13.Smiling and making new acquaintances

Smiling and making new acquaintances: a winning combination to create authentic connections and enrich our lives with memorable experiences. A smile is a universal gesture that transcends linguistic and cultural barriers, a way to communicate openness, sympathy, and willingness towards others. When we smile, we send a positive signal to our interlocutor, creating a climate of cordiality and promoting the establishment of a more genuine and sincere relationship.

A smile represents a bridge between people, a way to break the ice and create a relaxed and welcoming atmosphere. It is a form of non-verbal communication that conveys empathy and attracts the positive energies of the people we meet towards us. Smiling is contagious: often a serene look and a sincere smile are enough to melt resistance and gain the trust of those in front of us.

Making new acquaintances is an experience that enriches our lives and opens us up to new perspectives. Getting to know people different from us allows us to broaden our horizons, discover new passions and interests, and confront ourselves with viewpoints different from our own. Each encounter represents an opportunity to learn something new, to enrich our cultural and human baggage, to discover aspects of ourselves that we may not have known.

The process of mutual knowledge is an exciting journey that leads us to discover the hidden nuances of the people we meet, to share thoughts, emotions, and experiences, to build deep and meaningful bonds that enrich our existence. Each new acquaintance is a piece that adds to the mosaic of our life, contributing to make our path more varied and interesting.

Smiling and making new acquaintances is an art that must be cultivated with care and attention, with open-mindedness and readiness for confrontation. Every person we meet has something to teach us, something to give us, something to share with us. Just be willing to listen, to get involved, to be guided by curiosity and the desire to discover the world through the eyes of others.

Smiling is the key that opens the doors to people's hearts, fostering the establishment of a relationship of trust and complicity. Smiling is an act of kindness that costs nothing but can make a difference in the lives of those in front of us. A sincere smile is a precious gift that we can give every day, a sign of peace and harmony that contributes to creating an atmosphere of serenity and well-being around us.

Making new acquaintances pushes us to step out of our comfort zone, to open ourselves up to new experiences and discover unexplored worlds. Each encounter is a unique opportunity to learn something new, to enrich our knowledge base, to discover aspects of ourselves that we may not have known. Each person we meet is a piece of the puzzle of our life, a fundamental stage in our evolutionary path, an injection of freshness and vitality that prompts us to look to the future with confidence and optimism.

Smiling and making new acquaintances is an experience that enriches us internally, that opens us up to new opportunities and allows us to grow in a harmonious and balanced way. Each encounter is an opportunity to confront ourselves with viewpoints different from our own, to enrich our cultural and human baggage, to discover the beauty of diversity and the richness of otherness.

A smile is a gift we can give to ourselves and to others, an act of kindness that allows us to break down the barriers of indifference and selfishness, to create bridges of understanding and solidarity among people. Smiling is a way to communicate our love for life, our joy of living, our gratitude for the little things that make each day special.

Making new acquaintances opens us up to new horizons, allows us to explore new paths and seize opportunities that would otherwise have escaped us. Each person we meet is a universe to discover, a world to explore, a treasure to jealously guard in our hearts. Each new acquaintance is an opportunity to grow, to evolve, to become increasingly aware of ourselves and the world around us.

Smiling is the magical key that opens the doors to people's hearts, allowing us to connect with others and create authentic and lasting bonds. Smiling is a gesture of love towards ourselves and others, a way to express our gratitude for life and the people we meet along our journey. A smile is a universal language that transcends barriers of hatred and division, bringing us together in the name of beauty, goodness, and harmony.

Making new acquaintances is an extraordinary adventure that leads us to discover the beauty and complexity of being human, to share thoughts, emotions, and feelings with those in front of us, to build bridges of dialogue and understanding that withstand life's storms. Every encounter is an opportunity to learn something new, to grow internally, to enrich our repertoire of experiences and knowledge.

A smile is a gesture of peace and love that allows us to create harmony and beauty around us, to transform our relationships into rivers of light and joy. Smiling is an injection of beauty that revitalizes our hearts and fills us with positive energy, a signal of hope that urges us to look to the future with confidence and optimism. A smile is the mantra that accompanies us along our journey, the light that guides us through the dark night of doubts and uncertainties.

Making new acquaintances is an adventure that enriches us internally, that makes us grow and evolve, that pushes us to overcome our limits and discover our true selves. Every person we meet is an opportunity to learn something new, to challenge ourselves, to confront the different and the unknown. Every new acquaintance is a treasure that we treasure jealously in our hearts, a precious gem that accompanies us on our journey of growth and discovery.

Smiling is a gift that we can give to ourselves and others every day, an act of love and gratitude that warms the heart and illuminates the mind. Smiling is a way to transmit joy and happiness, to express our appreciation for the little things that make our existence unique. A smile is a universal language that transcends barriers of language and culture, allowing us to communicate with anyone, anywhere, at any time.

Making new acquaintances is an adventure

that enriches us internally, opens us up to new perspectives, and allows us to grow in a deep and authentic way. Every person we meet is an opportunity to learn something new, to enrich our repertoire of experiences, to discover sides of ourselves that we may not have known. Every new encounter is an opportunity to challenge ourselves, to confront ideas different from our own, to open our hearts and minds to the beauty and diversity of the world.

A smile is a gesture of generosity that allows us to give love and happiness to others, to share our joy of living with those in front of us, to transmit a message of peace and harmony that resonates in the hearts of those who receive it. Smiling is a way to express our gratitude for life and the people we meet along our journey, a way to show our respect and esteem for anyone we encounter on our path.

Making new acquaintances is an adventure that enriches us internally, opens us up to new perspectives, and allows us to grow in a harmonious and balanced way. Every person we meet is an opportunity to learn something new, to enrich our knowledge and experiences, to discover the hidden beauty of life and human nature. Every new encounter is a precious gift that we jealously guard within us, an endless source of inspiration and personal growth.

Smiling is a universal language that transcends language and culture barriers, allowing us to communicate with anyone, anywhere, at any time. Smiling is a gesture of love and kindness that brings people closer, creating an atmosphere of trust and harmony around us. A smile is a bridge of light that connects hearts and souls, fostering the establishment of authentic and deep relationships based on reciprocity and mutual understanding.

Making new acquaintances is an experience that enriches us internally, prompting us to look at the world with new eyes and discover the beauty and richness of human diversity. Every person we encounter is a universe to explore, a treasure to uncover, a friend to win over with the honesty and sincerity of our hearts. Every new encounter is an irreplaceable opportunity to grow, to evolve, to become more aware of ourselves and others.

A smile is a gift we can give to ourselves and others every day, a gesture of love and gratitude that allows us to radiate joy and happiness around us. Smiling is a way to communicate our joy of living, our gratitude for life and the people around us, a way to convey a message of peace and harmony that resonates in the hearts of those who receive it. A smile is a universal gift that enables us to establish authentic and deep connections with others, creating an atmosphere of understanding and solidarity that envelops people like a silent but intense embrace.

Making new acquaintances is an extraordinary adventure that leads us to discover the beauty and complexity of human beings, to share thoughts, emotions, and feelings with those in front of us, to build bridges of dialogue and understanding that withstand life's storms. Every encounter is an opportunity to learn something new, to grow internally, to enrich our experiences and knowledge. Every new acquaintance is a puzzle piece that adds to the mosaic of our lives, a precious part of the puzzle we are building day by day with patience and dedication.

A smile is the most powerful weapon we have to create authentic and lasting bonds with others, to transmit happiness and serenity to those in front of us, to radiate positivity and optimism around us. Smiling is a way to express our gratitude for life and the people we meet along our journey, to show our love and sympathy for everyone we encounter on our path. A smile is a ray of sunshine that brightens dark and stormy days, that makes hearts bloom in spring and turns tears into smiles of joy and emotion.

Making new acquaintances pushes us to overcome our limits and explore uncharted worlds, to test ourselves and confront ideas different from our own. Every person we meet is an opportunity to grow, to evolve, to broaden our horizons and discover new perspectives of growth and personal fulfillment. Every new encounter is a chance to open ourselves to the different and the unknown, to challenge ourselves and enrich our knowledge and experiences.

A smile is a universal language that speaks to the hearts of people, creating an atmosphere of trust and complicity between the one who smiles and the one who receives that smile. Smiling is a gesture of love and gratitude that allows us to transmit joy and happiness to others, creating an atmosphere of harmony and serenity around us. A smile is a sun that illuminates dark and stormy days, warms hearts, and illuminates minds with its delicate yet powerful light.

Making new acquaintances opens us up to new opportunities and allows us to grow in a balanced and harmonious way, to discover the hidden beauty of life and human nature. Every encounter is an opportunity to learn something new, to enrich our experiences and knowledge, to discover sides of ourselves that we may not have known. Every person we meet is a treasure that we jealously guard in our hearts, a friend who accompanies us on our journey of growth and discovery.

A smile is a song sung with the heart, a delicate and powerful melody that resonates through time and space, awakening the deepest and most authentic emotions we hold within us. Smiling is a way to express our gratitude for life and the people we meet along our path, to transmit our joy of living, our hope for the future, our trust in the power of love and compassion. A smile is a bridge of light that connects people's souls, uniting them in an invisible yet powerful embrace, guiding them towards light and peace.

Making new acquaintances is an experience that enriches our lives and opens us up to new perspectives of growth and personal fulfillment. Every person we meet is an opportunity to learn something new, to expand our horizons, to discover the beauty and complexity of human beings. Every new encounter is an opportunity to test ourselves, to confront ideas different from our own, to open our hearts and minds to the beauty and diversity of the world.

A smile is a gift we can give to others and ourselves every day, a gesture of love and gratitude that allows us to radiate joy and happiness around us. Smiling is a way to express our joy of living, our gratitude for life and the people around us, to convey a message of peace and harmony that resonates in the hearts of all who receive it.

14. The importance of friendship

Attending social events to meet new people is a common practice for those looking to expand their circle of friends and create new meaningful connections. This activity can lead to numerous opportunities for personal and professional growth, but it can also be an intimidating experience for many people. However, with the right mindset and strategies, it is possible to make the experience of attending social events much more enjoyable and rewarding.

First and foremost, it is important to have a positive and open approach towards social events. See them as an opportunity to meet new and interesting people, rather than as an obligation or imposition. Maintaining a positive attitude will make you more attractive and will allow people to approach you more easily.

A good strategy for meeting new people is to be proactive in establishing new relationships. Don't wait for others to start a conversation with you: actively try to engage people in interesting and stimulating conversations. Ask open-ended questions that can lead to deep discussions and share your opinions assertively but respectfully.

It is also important to be authentic and genuine in your interactions with others. Show your true self and do not be afraid to be vulnerable or show your emotions. People are attracted to those who are genuine and sincere, so don't hesitate to show your most authentic side.

Another useful strategy for meeting new people is to look for common ground or shared interests. Try to identify people who share your passions or have similar experiences to yours. This will make it easier to establish a bond and create a deeper connection with them.

Furthermore, it is important to pay attention to non-verbal communication. Body language can convey a lot of information about you and your personality, so make sure to be aware of your gestures, posture, and eye contact. Maintain an open and friendly attitude and always be respectful towards others.

Once you have started to make new acquaintances, it is important to keep the relationship alive. Exchange contacts and try to stay in touch with the people you have met at social events. Invite them for a coffee or an informal lunch to deepen mutual understanding and create a stronger connection.

Attending social events to meet new people can be a challenge for many people, but with the right mindset and strategies, it can become a very rewarding and enriching experience. Remember to be authentic, proactive, and attentive to non-verbal communication, and you will be able to create new meaningful and lasting connections with interesting and like-minded people.

15.Remain open to different types of friendships

Being open to different types of friendships means accepting and appreciating people for who they are, without making distinctions based on common interests, cultural backgrounds, or lifestyles. It is an approach that allows us to enrich ourselves personally and open ourselves up to new perspectives and experiences.

We often tend to surround ourselves with people similar to us, with the same passions and values, because we feel more comfortable and understood in the company of individuals who share our ideas. However, restricting ourselves to only relating to people similar to us can be limiting and prevent us from discovering new facets of life and society.

Friendships can be classified into different categories, from convenience friendships to deep and lasting ones. It is important to be aware of these differences and how each type of friendship can enrich our lives in different ways.

Convenience friendships are those that are formed out of necessity or simple common interests, such as school or workmates. These bonds may be superficial, but they can still bring moments of fun and mutual support. It is important not to underestimate them, as they can represent an important part of our social circle.

Transient friendships are those that are created at certain moments in our lives and may last for a limited period. They can be intense and meaningful bonds, but are destined to dissolve over time. These friendships can still teach us something important about ourselves and others, contributing to our personal growth.

True and deep friendships are based on mutual

understanding, respect, and support. These are bonds that withstand difficulties and distances, nurtured by sincerity and authenticity. These friendships are rare and precious, accompanying us throughout our lives, providing moments of joy and sharing.

Remaining open to different types of friendships means not closing ourselves off to new acquaintances and the possibility of creating meaningful bonds, regardless of their type. This involves being ready to welcome people for who they are, without judging or labeling them based on stereotypes or prejudices.

Being open to different types of friendships also means being willing to take risks and be surprised by others. Each of us has something unique to offer and teach others, and only by opening ourselves to new experiences can we enrich ourselves as individuals and grow.

The diversity of friendships allows us to broaden our horizons and engage with realities different from our own. This makes us more flexible, empathetic, and open to diversity, fundamental qualities in today's society. Through various types of friendships, we can learn to appreciate the richness of differences and overcome prejudices that prevent us from truly understanding others.

Furthermore, remaining open to different types of friendships allows us to expand our social network and access new opportunities and perspectives. The relationships we establish with others can open doors that would otherwise remain closed, allowing us to grow professionally and personally.

Being open to different types of friendships requires a certain amount of vulnerability and courage, as it means opening up to the risk of being hurt or disappointed. However, it is through this sincere and authentic exchange that we can find the true richness of human relationships and the true meaning of friendship.

To remain open to different types of friendships, it is important to cultivate some fundamental qualities, such as active listening and empathy. These qualities allow us to truly understand others, embrace their differences, and establish authentic and meaningful bonds.

It is also important to be willing to compromise and set aside pride to preserve a friendship. Every relationship has its ups and downs, and only through mutual trust and willingness to forgive can we overcome difficulties and strengthen our bonds with others.

Finally, it is important to remember that remaining open to different types of friendships does not mean accepting harmful behaviors or toxic relationships. It is essential to have the courage to set boundaries and distance ourselves from people who harm us, preserving our mental health and well-being.

Welcoming people for who they are, without prejudices or distinctions, allows us to open ourselves to new perspectives and experiences, enriching our lives with new colors and nuances. Only through the diversity of human relationships can we truly understand the world and discover the true meaning of friendship.

16. Tips for keeping friendship alive over time

Friendship is one of the most precious bonds we can have in life. It is a treasure that must be nurtured with care, attention, and dedication, so that it can last over time and withstand the challenges that life throws at us. Keeping a friendship alive over time is not always easy, but with commitment and awareness, it is possible. In this article, we will explore some practical tips on how to preserve and strengthen friendship bonds over the years.

The first fundamental tip for keeping friendship alive over time is communication. It is important to maintain an open and sincere dialogue with your friends, expressing your feelings, sharing your experiences, and actively listening to what your friends have to say. Communication is at the foundation of any human relationship and represents the glue that keeps friends together. One should never take for granted that the other person knows what we think or feel, but it is important to express thoughts and emotions clearly and honestly.

Furthermore, it is essential to ensure that communication is bilateral, meaning that both parties have the opportunity to express themselves and be listened to. It is important to be willing to listen to your friends without judging, interrupting, or giving unsolicited advice. Actively listening means being present in the moment and allowing the other person to express themselves freely, without feeling judged or interrupted. In this way, they will feel understood, accepted, and respected, creating a stronger and deeper bond between you.

Another important aspect of keeping friendship alive over time is mutual trust. Without trust, friendship cannot last long. It is important to trust your friends, believe in their words and actions, and ensure they can trust you in the same way. Trust is built over time through words and actions that demonstrate respect and affection for the other person. It is important to be honest, consistent, and reliable with your friends, so as not to disappoint the expectations they have of you. Being sincere and transparent with your friends helps to create an atmosphere of trust and mutual understanding, crucial for preserving friendship over time.

Furthermore, it is important to respect the differences and diversities that may exist between you. Each individual is unique and different from others, and it is natural for friends to have different opinions, tastes, and interests. It is important to accept and respect these differences, without trying to impose your opinions or change the other person. Respecting differences means accepting the other person for who they are, without judging or criticizing them, but appreciating their uniqueness and paying attention to their needs and desires. Accepting and valuing differences between you will make your friendship richer and based on a solid and lasting foundation.

Another important tip for keeping friendship alive over time is to dedicate quality time together. It is crucial to find time to be together, sharing enjoyable and fun moments that can strengthen the bond between you. Planning activities together, such as outings, dinners, trips, or simply a phone call chat, can help to maintain contact and strengthen friendship bonds over time. Spending time together is important for creating unforgettable memories that can consolidate the bond between you and renew the mutual affection that connects you.

Furthermore, it is crucial to be present in times of difficulty or need for your friends. Friendship is truly shown in difficult moments, when you are called upon to provide support, comfort, and assistance to your friends. It is important to be available to listen, support, and console your friends when they need it, without shying away from the challenges they may face. Being present and supportive in times of difficulty helps to strengthen the bond of trust and affection between you, creating a stronger and deeper connection that can withstand the tests of time.

Finally, another important recommendation for keeping friendship alive over time is to be willing to forgive and apologize when mistakes are made or when harm is caused to the other. Nobody is perfect, and mistakes can happen, like saying the wrong things or behaving inappropriately towards others. It is important to be humble and courageous in acknowledging your mistakes and apologizing when you are in the wrong, showing that you are willing to repair the damage caused and restore harmony in the relationship. Likewise, it is important to be ready to forgive your friends when they make mistakes, without harboring grudges or resentment, but with a spirit of understanding and mutual acceptance. Forgiveness is a gesture of great generosity and humanity that helps to heal wounds and restore trust and affection between you.

Keeping friendship alive over time requires commitment, attention, and dedication from both parties. It is essential to communicate clearly and sincerely, maintain a relationship based on mutual trust, respect differences, dedicate quality time together, be present in times of difficulty, and be willing to forgive and apologize when mistakes are made. By following these tips and showing love, respect, and gratitude towards your friends, it will be possible to preserve and strengthen friendship bonds over the years, creating unbreakable and lasting bonds that will enrich our lives and hearts.

17.Facing envy and jealousy in friendship

Envy and jealousy are two negative feelings that can heavily impact a friendship. When one of these feelings arises within a friendship, it can lead to tensions, conflicts, and emotional distance. Handling these feelings in a wise and mature way is essential in order to preserve the relationship and maintain a healthy and genuine bond with the dear person.

Before addressing envy and jealousy in friendship, it is important to understand the difference between the two emotions. While envy arises when one desires something a friend has and feels a sense of lack or inferiority in comparison, jealousy stems from the fear of losing the friendship due to another person or situation. Both feelings can be harmful if not handled properly, leading to negative behaviors such as rivalry, constant criticism, or emotional detachment.

To address envy and jealousy in friendship, it is crucial to be aware of one's own feelings and reactions. Often, jealousy and envy can stem from personal insecurities or past negative experiences. Taking the time to reflect on what triggers these feelings and what one's fears are can help better understand the reason behind these emotions and find positive ways to address them.

Once the roots of envy and jealousy are understood, it is important to communicate openly and honestly with the friend involved. Talking about one's emotions and fears can help dispel misunderstandings and create an atmosphere of trust and mutual understanding. It is important to do so in a respectful and non-accusatory manner, avoiding blaming the other person and trying to find solutions together.

In some cases, it might be helpful to involve a mediator or therapist to address envy and jealousy in friendship. A qualified professional can help explore the dynamics of the relationship, identify underlying issues, and find effective strategies to overcome negative feelings and strengthen the bond between friends.

Furthermore, it is important to work on oneself to overcome envy and jealousy in friendship. Working on self-esteem, empathy, and self-acceptance can help reduce feelings of envy and jealousy and promote a healthier and positive relationship with others. Additionally, practicing gratitude for what one has and focusing on one's passions and interests can help focus on what makes one happy rather than comparing oneself to others.

Lastly, it is important to understand that envy and jealousy are common human feelings and there is nothing wrong with experiencing them. What matters is how these feelings are addressed and managed within a friendship. Facing envy and jealousy in a mature and compassionate way can help strengthen the bond with friends and promote greater intimacy and mutual trust.

Overcoming these negative feelings can lead to more authentic, deep, and satisfying relationships with friends, creating lasting and meaningful emotional connections.

18.The importance of mutual support among friends

The importance of mutual support among friends is a fundamental and essential theme for every person's life. Friends are those who support us in times of difficulty, help us overcome challenges, and stand by us in our decisions. They are an integral part of our lives and without them, we would be lost.

Mutual support among friends is based on a bond of trust, respect, and affection. They are the ones who know us better than anyone else and are ready to lend a hand when needed. Mutual support among friends is a form of solidarity that is expressed through concrete acts of help and comfort.

When we talk about mutual support among friends, we mean the ability to be there for each other in every moment, both in times of joy and in times of sadness. Friends are those who support us when we are weak, encourage us when we are unsure, and motivate us when we are tired. They are our rock that we can always rely on.

Mutual support among friends is also essential for our emotional and psychological well-being. Friends are those who listen to us without judging, provide honest advice, and help us find solutions to our problems. They make us feel welcomed and loved, creating a positive and constructive environment around us.

Furthermore, mutual support among friends allows us to grow and improve as individuals. Friends challenge us to push our limits, question ourselves, and see things from different perspectives. They help us develop our skills and discover new sides of ourselves that we didn't know existed.

Mutual support among friends is also essential

for our mental health. Friends are the ones who make us laugh when we are sad, distract us when we are stressed, and reassure us when we are anxious. They are an antidote to loneliness and help us feel less isolated and more integrated into society.

But mutual support among friends is not just about taking, but also giving. Being a good friend means being available, empathetic, and generous with others. It means listening without interrupting, offering help without expecting anything in return, and being there when others need us.

Mutual support among friends is based on a reciprocity of actions and feelings that must be nurtured over time. It is fueled through the sharing of experiences, reciprocal help, and sincere intentions. Friends enrich our lives and make us feel part of something bigger than ourselves.

They are an invaluable source of support that helps us overcome life's difficulties and grow as individuals. Friends are the pillars we can always rely on, supporting us in dark times and accompanying us along the journey of life. Therefore, it is essential to cultivate friendships, be there for others, and contribute to the happiness and well-being of our friends.

19.Create unforgettable memories with friends

Creating unforgettable memories with friends is one of the most beautiful goals to achieve in life. Friends are those who share special moments with us, support us during difficult times, and make us smile even when it feels like the world is falling apart. That is why it is important to invest time and energy in building strong and lasting bonds with the people who are most important to us.

But how can unforgettable memories be created with friends? First of all, it is essential to have a group of friends with similar interests to ours. In fact, it is much easier to create unforgettable memories when sharing a passion for the same activities. Whether it's traveling, playing sports, cooking, or simply spending time together chatting, having common interests that allow for a deep and lasting bond is important.

One of the best ideas for creating unforgettable memories with friends is to organize trips together. Traveling is an experience that allows you to discover new places, different cultures, and live intense emotions. Planning a trip with friends can be an excellent opportunity to strengthen bonds and create memories that will be etched in your memory forever. Whether it's a weekend in the mountains, a beach vacation, or a tour exploring European capitals, traveling with friends is an experience that you will definitely not easily forget.

Another idea for creating unforgettable memories with friends is to organize special evenings. Whether it's a dinner at home, a night at the movies, or a party at a club, spending time together in a different way than usual can be a great opportunity to create unique and irreplaceable memories. In addition, organizing special evenings with friends allows you to break away from the daily routine and have fun together in a more informal and relaxed setting.

Another idea for creating unforgettable memories with friends is to engage in outdoor activities. Whether it's taking a mountain hike, going mountain biking, or organizing a picnic in the countryside, spending time outdoors with friends is an experience that allows you to live intense emotions and create unforgettable memories. Furthermore, engaging in outdoor activities with friends allows you to enjoy the beauty of nature and strengthen the bond with the people we love.

Finally, another idea for creating unforgettable memories with friends is to do unusual and fun activities together. Whether it's taking a cooking class, organizing a themed party, or attending a concert, choosing unusual and fun activities to do with friends is a great way to experience intense emotions and create memories that will be etched in your memory forever. Additionally, engaging in unusual and fun activities with friends allows you to have fun together and create unique and irreplaceable moments.

Friends are indeed the people who support us, help us, and make us smile in the most difficult times. That is why it is important to invest time and energy in building strong and lasting bonds with the people who are most important to us. Whether it's organizing trips together, having special evenings, engaging in outdoor activities, or doing unusual and fun activities, it is essential to focus on the importance of human relationships and the value of the bonds that unite us with friends. Only in this way will it be possible to create unforgettable memories that will be etched in your memory forever.

20.The positive effect of friendships on mental and physical health

Friendships are an essential element in everyone's life and have a significant impact on our mental and physical health. The positive effect of friendship relationships on our well-being has been the subject of numerous studies and research over the years, demonstrating how important it is to cultivate meaningful bonds with those around us.

Friendships are often seen as a source of fun, emotional support, and experience sharing, but their impact on our health goes beyond these superficial aspects. Friendship relationships can positively influence our mental health by providing a sense of belonging, security, and support, which are essential elements for maintaining emotional and psychological balance.

One of the most evident effects of friendships

on mental health is the reduction of stress and anxiety. Spending time with friends, sharing thoughts and emotions, and receiving support in times of difficulty can help reduce stress levels and promote greater inner serenity. Friends act as valuable emotional support and can help us overcome life's challenges with greater resilience and optimism.

Additionally, friendships can contribute to improving our self-esteem and self-confidence. Feeling accepted, appreciated, and loved by our friends can increase confidence in our abilities and self-efficacy, fostering a more positive view of ourselves and our capabilities. This can have a significant impact on mental health, reducing the risk of mood disorders and promoting greater emotional stability.

Furthermore, friendships can enhance socialization and a sense of belonging to a group, which are fundamental elements for psychological well-being. Spending time with friends, participating in social activities, and sharing leisure moments can reduce feelings of loneliness and isolation, two risk factors for mental health. Friends allow us to experience a sense of community and social bonding, which are essential for our emotional and psychological health.

But the positive influence of friendships is not limited to the mental sphere, but also extends to our physical health. Numerous studies have shown that friendship relationships can have a significant impact on our body's health, influencing immunity, blood pressure, disease risk, and even longevity.

Friendship relationships can reduce stress, which is one of the main risk factors for various physical ailments. Chronic stress can weaken the immune system and increase the risk of cardiovascular, metabolic, and autoimmune diseases. Spending time with friends, laughing together, and sharing pleasant moments can reduce cortisol levels, the stress hormone, and promote greater physical resistance.

Moreover, friendships can positively influence our perception of well-being and happiness, which in turn can impact our physical health. Feeling loved, appreciated, and supported by our friends can promote the production of endorphins and other wellbeing-related neurotransmitters, helping to reduce the risk of depression, anxiety, and other psychological conditions.

Sharing pleasant experiences with friends, such as playing sports together, taking outdoor walks, or simply spending time together, can promote an active and healthy lifestyle, reducing the risk of obesity, diabetes, heart disease, and other lifestyle-related illnesses.

Furthermore, friendships can have a positive impact on our cognitive health, fostering mental stimulation and socialization.

Maintaining active friendship relationships involves communication, idea exchange, and thought sharing, which can promote greater cognitive development and mental flexibility. Additionally, emotional support and experience sharing can enhance our problem-solving abilities and adaptation to life's challenges.

Lastly, friendships can contribute to promoting a healthy and balanced lifestyle, encouraging us to take care of ourselves and adopt healthy habits. Friends can be a valuable support in our dietary choices, physical exercise, and maintaining a balance between work and personal life, providing us with motivation, support, and encouragement in our lifestyle choices.

Friendships play a fundamental role in promoting overall well-being, positively influencing both mental and physical health. Cultivating meaningful and deep friendship relationships can be a valuable ally in maintaining emotional and psychological balance, reducing stress, promoting socialization, and fostering a healthy and active lifestyle. For these reasons, it is important to invest time and energy in our friendship relationships, taking care of our connections and cultivating authentic and meaningful relationships with those around us.

21.Being empathetic and understanding with friends

Being empathetic and understanding towards friends is one of the fundamental bases for maintaining healthy and lasting relationships. Empathy is the ability to put oneself in someone else's shoes, to understand their emotions and feelings without judging. Being empathetic means being able to see things from the other person's perspective, to understand what they are going through, and to show solidarity and support.

On the other hand, being understanding means accepting and respecting others' differences, listening to them without judging or criticizing, and trying to understand their motivations and actions. Being understanding allows for creating a climate of trust and open communication, promoting the growth and development of relationships.

But why is it so important to be empathetic and understanding towards our friends? How can these qualities positively influence relationships and contribute to making them more fulfilling and meaningful? And how can we develop and cultivate empathy and understanding in our friendships?

Let's start with empathy. Being empathetic towards our friends means being able to recognize and respect their feelings, being there for them when they need support, and listening to them without judgment. Empathy allows for creating a deep and authentic bond with others, making them feel welcomed and understood.

An empathetic friend can put themselves in the other person's shoes, can perceive the emotional nuances of a situation, and can offer support sincerely and genuinely. This creates a climate of trust and openness, allowing both friends to share their emotions and face life challenges and difficulties together.

Being empathetic towards our friends also means being able to recognize when they need help or support and being willing to offer it without hesitation. An empathetic friend is always available to listen, console, and support, without expecting anything in return but simply because they genuinely care about the other person's well-being.

Empathy is a bridge that connects two people, allowing them to overcome the barriers of diversity and create deep and meaningful relationships. Being empathetic towards our friends also means being able to accept their differences and peculiarities, to respect their choices, and to appreciate their unique qualities.

But empathy alone is not enough. Being understanding is equally important for maintaining healthy and positive relationships. Being understanding towards our friends means accepting them for who they are, with their strengths and flaws, and respecting them in their choices and decisions.

Being understanding allows for creating a climate of mutual respect, in which everyone has the freedom to express themselves and be themselves without fear of being judged or criticized. A understanding friend can understand the other person's motivations and emotions, offer support and advice without imposing their own point of view.

Being understanding towards our friends also means being able to forgive and overcome misunderstandings that may arise during a relationship. A understanding friend can set aside pride and anger, try to understand the other person's perspective, and always try to find a compromise that can satisfy both parties.

But how can we develop and cultivate

empathy and understanding in our friendships? Here are some practical tips to become more empathetic and understanding towards our friends:

1. Actively listen: learn to listen with attention and without interruptions, giving space to the other person to express their emotions and thoughts.

2. Put yourself in the other person's shoes: try to imagine how the other person would feel in a certain situation and try to understand their emotions and feelings.

3. Show support and solidarity: when a friend needs help or support, be available and present, offering your support sincerely and genuinely.

4. Accept differences: learn to accept the other person's differences, respecting their choices

and opinions even if you do not share them.

5. Be patient and understanding: accept that each person is different and show patience and understanding when difficulties or misunderstandings arise.

In conclusion, being empathetic and understanding towards our friends is essential for maintaining healthy and lasting relationships. Empathy allows us to put ourselves in the other person's shoes, to understand their emotions, and to offer our support sincerely and genuinely. Understanding, on the other hand, allows us to accept and respect the other person's differences, to listen to them without judgment, and to create a climate of mutual trust.

Cultivating empathy and understanding in our friendships allows us to create deep and meaningful bonds, offering each other support, understanding, and solidarity. Always remember to listen, respect, and accept our friends for who they are, showing them that we are present and willing to support them at all times.

22.Managing the distance between friends

Managing the various distances between friends is a challenge that many people face throughout their lives. Physical, geographic, or emotional distance can significantly impact the relationships between friends, but it is important to find ways to address and overcome these challenges to maintain a strong and lasting bond.

Physical distance is one of the most common forms of separation between friends, which can result from reasons such as moving to a different city, studying or working abroad, or simply life taking two people in different directions. This type of distance can create a tangible barrier between friends, but there are several strategies that can help keep the bond alive despite the distance.

One of the first things to do to manage physical distance between friends is to establish a method of regular and consistent communication. Thanks to modern technology, it is easier than ever to stay in touch with friends even miles apart. Using instant messaging applications, video calls, and social media can help reduce the feeling of loneliness and isolation that often accompanies physical distance.

Moreover, scheduling visits or vacations together can be a great way to strengthen the bond between friends and create new memories together. Although it may be expensive or require organization, spending quality face-to-face time is essential to maintain a strong relationship despite the distance.

In addition to physical distance, geographic distance can pose a challenge for friendships. Being separated by thousands of miles can make it difficult to maintain a close and meaningful bond, but there are strategies that can help manage this form of distance.

One of the most important things to do to manage geographic distance between friends is to be aware of differences in time zones and daily routines. Respecting each other's time and life rhythms can help avoid misunderstandings and tensions in communication, allowing for an open and honest dialogue despite the distance.

Furthermore, using digital tools such as shared calendars and time management apps can facilitate the planning of calls, video calls, or virtual meetings, allowing for a constant connection despite physical distance. Additionally, writing letters or sending gifts via traditional mail can be a romantic and personal way to show affection and care for a faraway friend.

Finally, emotional distance can be one of the most complex challenges to face in managing friendships. Emotional distance can stem from communication issues, lack of trust, or simply from the separate growth and evolution of two people. However, it is possible to overcome this form of distance with commitment, sincerity, and mutual respect.

One of the first things to do to manage emotional distance between friends is to be honest and open about your feelings and thoughts. Communicating clearly and honestly can help overcome misunderstandings and resentments, allowing you to address issues head-on and strengthen the connection between friends.

Moreover, it is important to show empathy and understanding towards the other person, trying to put yourself in their shoes and understand their motivations and concerns. Showing genuine interest in the other person's life and feelings can help strengthen the emotional bond between friends and overcome any obstacles that may threaten it.

Finally, dedicating quality time together and

participating in meaningful experiences can help emotionally reconnect and create new memories to share. Supporting each other in difficult times and celebrating successes and achievements together can strengthen the bond between friends and create a solid foundation for a lasting and fulfilling relationship.

Managing the distance between friends is a challenge that may require commitment, communication, and understanding from both parties. Whether the distance is physical, geographic, or emotional, it is important to find ways to maintain a strong and meaningful bond despite the difficulties. With sincerity, respect, and dedication, it is possible to overcome the challenges of distance and maintain a deep and cherished relationship over time.

23. Rewarding friends with acts of kindness and appreciation

Rewarding friends with acts of kindness and appreciation is a wonderful way to show how much we value the relationships we have with the people around us. Friends are a fundamental part of our lives, sharing moments of joy, sadness, success, and failure with us. It is important, therefore, to show our gratitude and appreciation for their constant support and presence in our lives.

There are many ways to reward friends with acts of kindness and appreciation, and each one can make a difference in strengthening and consolidating the bonds that connect us to our loved ones. Kindness and appreciation can be expressed in multiple ways, from the simple gesture of saying "thank you" for a favor received, to organizing a special surprise to show how much we care about the people in our lives.

One of the most effective ways to reward friends with kindness is to take the time to listen to them and show interest in what they are experiencing and thinking. Often, in our hectic lives, we neglect to pay attention and actively listen to the people around us. Being available and willing to listen to our friends is a fundamental act of kindness that can make a difference in strengthening the bond we share with them.

Furthermore, it is important to show appreciation for the qualities and virtues of our friends, emphasizing what we admire about them and recognizing their abilities and talents. Many times, we take for granted the positive qualities of the people close to us, without realizing how important it is to show appreciation for what they do and who they are. Recognizing the merits of our friends is a kind gesture that will not only make them feel valued but will also strengthen the trust and friendship that binds us to them.

In addition to active listening and recognizing the qualities of our friends, we can reward them with concrete acts of kindness and appreciation. A simple but meaningful way to show our affection and gratitude is to send a thank-you message, a handwritten note, or a small symbolic gift to let them know how much we value their presence in our lives. Even a daily act of kindness, such as making a cup of hot tea for our favorite friend or offering a hug in times of difficulty, can make a difference in conveying our affection and appreciation for them.

Furthermore, organizing a special outing or a surprise dinner to celebrate a friend's birthday or an important milestone is a wonderful way to show how much we care about them. Planning a night out together, a picnic in the park, or a dinner at home can be acts of kindness and appreciation that create unforgettable memories and strengthen the bond we share with our friends.

Another idea to reward friends with kindness and appreciation is to involve them in activities that make them happy and fulfilled. Organizing a relaxing day at the spa, a trip to the beach, or a night at the movies can be perfect ways to show our friends how much we care about their well-being and happiness. Additionally, sharing common passions and interests, such as attending a course together or participating in a sports competition, can strengthen friendship bonds and create moments of joy and shared enjoyment.

Finally, a precious way to reward friends with acts of kindness and appreciation is to be present in times of need and difficulty. Showing solidarity and being available when a friend is going through a tough time, offering emotional and practical support without judging or criticizing, can make the difference in making the loved one feel accepted and understood. Being a safe and reliable point of reference for our friends in moments of crisis or suffering is an act of kindness and appreciation that is priceless and can further cement the bond we share with them.

Rewarding friends with acts of kindness and appreciation is a powerful way to strengthen friendships and show how much we value the presence of loved ones in our lives. Kindness and appreciation are fundamental values that enrich human relationships and create lasting and meaningful bonds. Showing gratitude and affection for our friends through concrete and sincere gestures is a wonderful way to express the love and appreciation we feel for them, and to create unforgettable memories of shared experiences and growth together.

24.Organizing trips / vacations with friends

Organizing trips/vacations with friends is an exciting and fun experience that requires good planning and coordination. Sharing moments of relaxation and adventure with friends can create unforgettable memories and strengthen the bonds between people. In this article, we will explore some useful tips on how to organize trips and vacations with friends, so that everything goes smoothly and you can have an unforgettable experience.

The first thing to do when deciding to organize a trip with friends is to choose the destination. It is important that there is consensus among all participants, to avoid possible problems or disagreements during the trip. It is useful to discuss each other's interests and preferences and try to find a destination that can please everyone a little. For example, if some prefer the mountains and others the sea, you can opt for a destination that offers both options, such as the Balearic

Islands or the Maritime Alps.

Once the destination is chosen, it is important to set the dates of the trip in advance, to allow everyone to organize themselves with their commitments and book any days off or work permits. Furthermore, it is useful to establish a common budget and decide how the costs of the trip will be divided, from transportation to accommodations, meals to activities to do. It is important that everyone is transparent about their financial possibilities, in order to avoid unpleasant discussions later on.

Once everyone agrees on the destination, dates, and budget, you can proceed with booking flights or the chosen mode of transportation. It is advisable to make reservations well in advance, to take advantage of more advantageous rates and have the opportunity to choose the most convenient solutions. Additionally, it is important to keep in mind that seats on planes and trains can fill up quickly, so it is best not to wait too long.

Once the logistical issues related to transportation are resolved, you can proceed with the search for accommodation. There are several options available, from vacation rentals to hotels, bed and breakfasts to hostels, and the choice will depend on the preferences of all participants. It is important to establish the type of preferred accommodation from the start and look for solutions that can meet everyone's needs, from comfort to location. Furthermore, it is advisable to book accommodation well in advance, especially during the tourist season, to avoid availability issues and excessively high prices.

Once all the logistical details have been resolved, it's time to think about the activities to do during the trip. It is useful to make a list of the main attractions of the chosen destination and discuss them with friends, to decide which things everyone likes the most and organize a program that can please everyone a little. It is important to leave room for relaxation and improvisation, in order to fully enjoy the trip without feeling too constrained by a rigid schedule.

During the trip, it is important to maintain good communication and cooperation among all participants. It is normal that there may be inconveniences or problems during the trip, but it is important to address them calmly and try to find solutions together. It is useful to listen to everyone's opinions and try to find a compromise that satisfies everyone's needs, in order to avoid possible conflicts and tensions within the group.

Finally, it is important to remember that the main goal of organizing trips and vacations with friends is to have fun and create special memories together. Despite difficulties and unforeseen events along the way, it is important to maintain a positive and open attitude, and appreciate the experiences and emotions that will be shared with friends. In fact, traveling with friends can be a unique opportunity to share moments of joy, adventure, and growth together, and strengthen the bonds between people.

Organizing trips and vacations with friends can be an unforgettable and fun experience, which requires a good amount of planning, cooperation, and flexibility. By following the tips described here and working together as a team, you can experience an extraordinary trip, full of special moments and surprises. So, what are you waiting for? Pack your bags, call your friends, and embark on an adventure, because the best trips are those shared with the people we love. Have a great trip!

Index

www.ingramcontent.com/pod-product-compliance
Lightning Source LLC
Chambersburg PA
CBHW061649250726
48659CB00004B/1426